BLOOD SONGS

BLOOD SONGS

poems

October 9, 2000 – April 3, 2001

Daniel Abdal-Hayy Moore

The Ecstatic Exchange

2012
Philadelphia

For quotes any longer than those for critical articles and reviews,
contact:
The Ecstatic Exchange,
6470 Morris Park Road, Philadelphia, PA 19151-2403
email: abdalhayy@danielmoorepoetry.com

First Edition
ISBN: 978-0-578-10678-6 (paper)
Published by *The Ecstatic Exchange*,
6470 Morris Park Road, Philadelphia, PA 19151-2403

Also available from The Ecstatic Exchange:
Knocking from Inside, poems by Tiel Aisha Ansari

Acknowledgments: The poems *The Predicament* and *The Practice of Ecstasy*
won the Nazim Hikmet Poetry Prize for 2012, and were published in the
Festival chapbook

Front cover collage by the author,
back cover photograph by Mehmet Oztürk

بسم الله الرحمن الرحيم

DEDICATION

To
Shaykh ibn al-Habib
(and the continuation of the Habibiyya)
Shaykh Bawa Muhaiyuddeen,
all shuyukh of instruction and ma'arifa,
to
Baji Tayyaba Khanum
of the unsounded depths

All seekers, setter-outers and arrivers
wherever on whatever Path to
Allah's Glory and Success

And to my beloved wife Malika
our lovely long life together

———

The earth is not bereft
of Light

CONTENTS

AUTHOR'S INTRODUCTION

I'm really not sure why this particular collection of my poems is called *Blood Songs*, the title it has had since beginning the first poem of the book written in October of 2000, and though, as with other titles of mine, not necessarily threading a theme throughout, yet the title stands notwithstanding... and so it stands.

Poetic inspiration has always been a puzzle, from first oracles or seers when pampas grasses were blowing and mastodons roamed, to our prize-winning poets in their university offices and writery nooks, suddenly flashing and scribbling, or brow-wrinkling and calling up from Freudian or Jungian, Buddhist or Sufi or every other possible depths, these fragile and resilient linguistic exhalations. Where does it all come from? And... why do we do it? I've often thought of all the poems between published covers or secreted in drawers that cost the heart's blood of their scribes and yet go unread and unfelt by anyone else on earth forever. Other *Paradise Losts*, other *Tyger Tygers*, their Emily Dickinsons never known by anyone, even as eccentric or reclusive, like Henry Darger whose epic tomes were found after his death piled to the ceiling, minutely scribed and illustrated.

But these poems come in a wave, a waft, a raft of light, a sighting from afar that comes in near, like the whiskers of a cat when they kiss us, and tickle us with their sensitive feelers. Only it's a mouth in the heart, those phantom Cocteau lips speaking, and we only bend down our hearts as close as we can to hear. And we who write these down, in the language of our tribes, only telegraphing along the line what's in all our hearts, every man woman and child of us — or is that the poet's narcissitic conceit? Polishing the common linguistic coin to a higher luster. And in the eagerest intention, to get closer, somehow, absurdly perhaps, unembarrasedly, to God.

As for the collages on the covers of my Ecstatic Exchange Books, where control over the pictorial matter moves in serendipitous steps, things falling into place from near and far as in the listening of the poem, finding a basic photographic piece for a collage (something with perhaps open space, or evocative landscape, etc.) and then taking leads from its colors, shapes and imagery into the spinning world of meanings, I give up self-direction as much as possible — in the case of a poem, to listen, and in the case of a collage, to watch, wait, and pounce! Carve with a knife, paste with a glue stick, stand back and hope for the best... Heart's blood in extending out beyond the known, with patient anticipation to accept the light of astonishment.

I've favored the collage to most represent what I hope the poems also convey, an ecstatic believer's delight in this and the next world, in which many things happen at once and with a thrilling sure but seeming haphazardness, and a glorifying of the Master of both and all worlds, may He be praised, of which all else before His Face is simply a transparent mirage.

Mirage Collage... ah, a bell ringing!

Graceful death, who puts on its spotted robe when it goes to its victim,
playful killer whose loving embrace splits the antelope's heart.
                                        — *African poem*

Were the boon companions to look on its jar,
the seal would intoxicate them.
Were they to sprinkle it on a person's grave,
the spirit would return, and the body would quicken.
Were they to cast a seriously ill man in the shade of its vine's wall,
the illness would leave him.
Were they to carry a cripple near its tavern, he would walk.
And mutes, at the recollection of its taste, would speak.
Were its fragrance to waft in the East,
and in the West was a person with a stopped nose, he would smell.
                    — *Ibn Farid (from The Khamriyya, or Wine Ode*
                        translation by Raymond Farrin)

I'VE SAT LONG ENOUGH

I've sat long enough in the burning corner of the world
O my heart and seen foreign invaders put on masks of
authority over natural inhabitants

Where is justice where is the loudly ringing bell that will
stop this where is God's zigzag golden ray that comes
down on iniquity to burn it entirely away?

The column of flame in my own corner rises and
twists into a braid whose strands are
black and red

My eyes bulge as if ready to pop from their sockets
my mouth puckers as if the "O" it sounds will
put out the world's incessant flickering

When it finally subsides again I see the exact
same things as before except in place of humans I see
rhinoceroses and stinky bears giant slobbering iguanas and
jackals with razor sharp teeth tearing at each other
and laughing their heads off

Out of a column of smoke a hand emerges with a
cool goblet of water to slake the thirst of the victims
if they will only take it and drink

I myself am waiting for wine
and for my own flames to subside

and the smoke to turn into a crystalline
screen of clear vision

to walk through to the truth

10/9

THERE'S A SUBVERSIVE ELEMENT

There's a subversive element in every gathering
a wired informer in every convocation

a spy in every conversation touching on delicate issues
a betrayer whenever the space elevates to the level of the higher
raptors

There's an ear in every mouth connected to a
counter-network operated by hidden assailants

There's an eye in every close encounter or each time one
soul seems to touch the still pond of another and make
perfect pebble rings ripple concentrically from the center
everything waiting for the moment to rise up
and accuse the isolated instant taken from the continuous flow
and hit it against the present moment until it chimes and
gives up its secret for everyone with no
interest in its intrinsic beauty to witness
in the worst possible light

But the black arts never overcome the silver thread of
true resonance completely even if it only hangs suspended in
space for a second before it's
engulfed by dark's gargantuan maw

And finally eyes radiate calm
hearts beat with the regularity of
ocean waters in hidden tropical lagoons

The frail turn out to be the strong in the end
and the ferocious end up crying like babies for want of
more food

10/10

IF SOMETHING SHOULD SPEAK TO ME

If something should speak to me out of the air
(bring those mics in a little closer Lord)
and I heard the rustling of wings
and felt the sweetness or shocked awe that
such a visitation brings

and I was lying on my bed or sitting
by a dark window deep in a book or
strolling by a stream
and maybe it was accompanied by a
playful golden beam

(though I'm not so certain I'd require all these
added things but just that voice from the
first speaking out of the air to me and
me in conscious mode)

Ah Lord such an exquisite universe run so
smoothly and keenly
everything animated just so and mostly
invisibly or else we'd be
unable to act so freely

If a voice came to me thus out of sheer
immateriality
and no ventriloquism except God's own
ventriloquism across yawning canyons of
time/space

Ah Lord bring those mics in a little closer
and my ears and innermost heart

make
Oh so much purer!

10/12

LET THE SNAKE WHO KNOWS THE SECRET

Let the snake who knows the secret of
standing on two legs speak if he can

The elephant who knows the secret of
crouching so low nobody notices him in the
grass

Let the flame who knows the secret of the coolness of
running water speak if it dares

Or the water who flows into
any available form speak of the
scorching heat that comes of burning

What do we know who wear black in snow
and white as we slide into death?

How can we raise our voices filled with words
while a cold wind blows?

I want to stand up to my knees in God's ocean
and let tidal waves of His love lurch over me

Stop measuring the ocean itself with my
withering skeletal frame of 5 foot 10

the mountain peak of glittering glass with my
telescope from the Dollar Store

Unless our shoes are filled with blood we
haven't walked

Unless our cheeks are cliffs for tears
our hearts are only halfway home or
less

And the long snake of night is hanging from a
low bough

And the distant fire
may not warm our fingertips

TINY ZEBRAS OF THOUGHT

Tiny zebras of thought patter across the plain
a Thelonious Monk tune in my head as I
awake

This an homage poem to everyone who's ever
written a poem

Such clatter such tornado winds ripping doors off hinges
flinging them like frozen flying carpets across a
black sky to no lands of wonder

Destruction of existing structures before new
dwellings can be built in which
the Prince of Aquitane and the Princess and the Frog may live
along with the Ogre of Flame who burns the
dinner each time they sit down to eat
the Mascot of Water who then floods the food and makes it
inedible sun and moon in their
alternating minuet of day and night coming together with
uttermost formality the way
cells and microbes are formally kept separate
unless all hell breaks loose

I've left the floor before the band's begun
though no one notices the potted palms perhaps
the hat check girl who's been
looking after my head

Look away dear sister
the screwing back on ain't pretty

and the cabs are all made of ice out there
in Bone Land

10/20

SAD LITTLE FOLK

Sad little folk under skeletal umbrellas
we should turn in our *Self-Pity* licenses
and our *Me-First* buttons

and that awful gauze of *Look-At-Me* we
wrap around ourselves on all occasions

and the flaps on our ears that
keep us from actually listening

and the heavy gates on our hearts the ones with the
combination locks but no-one ever gets the
combination right

and we should finally give up the synthetic
coonskin caps of prolonged infantility
and turn down to inaudible the
loudspeakers of *No-One-Really-Understands-Me*
that are cunningly set to face just us though occasionally
we force someone else to listen to them too

And get rid of the too-small jacket of *Things-Would-Be-Better-If-Only*
and the wet noodles on our faces of
No-One-Really-Even-Cares that have
dried to the consistency of masks
that pass for faces to the general population

And stop pedaling the bicycle of

I'm-On-A-One-Way-Trip-To-Hell-So-don't-Call-Out-To-Me
As-I-Careen-Down-The-Hill

O all of these things!

And be instead a
waterbead on a bud

a wind of winter's storm

a perfect example of God's ingredients well-mixed

a whistling on the trestle

a light at the end of our own tunnels

a slow swoon

an extinguished moth
in the light of a greater flame

10/21

DUMBFOUNDED AND DISMAYED

Dumbfounded and dismayed and yet
not a one can stop it
raising a finger to stem a cascade
calling with thin voice over the roar of a waterfall of falling
buildings and the debris of millennia past

A tiny firefly of intermittent glimmer flitters by
the light like a drunk trying to light a match
against a wall of rock
and so takes heart
and now calls out and is silent
raises a hand then
drops it

I think an earthquake was about to
split us apart the other day
leaving all the celestially inspired on one side
all the terrestrially weighed down on the
other

But one word perfectly articulated on wingéd lips
held it in place like a room full of
unruly children
with fiery eyes and sharp teeth breathing heavily
little steam puffs

All the old trees are still standing
and we're still an intermixture of demon and

delight angel and anger waltzing with

jaggedy ease in a
raggedy moonlight

10/23

ONE DAY THE OCEAN

One day the ocean asked the shore:
"How come I keep beating on you but you
never answer?"

The shore remained silent but the sky responded by
pouring down rain

Then the rain asked the ocean
"How come I fall into you but you never seem to
rise?"

The ocean continued rolling but the sun above the
rain shone as heartily as ever its light waves stretching
186,000 miles per second and yet

rain clouds massed together and made
rain the ocean pounded on the
door of the shore with no
reply for another few thousand years

the shore hunkered down on the earth like a mammal cub on its
mother's back as it
roved around its axis rowing itself through space
like an empty canoe whose

everywhere is its Master Rower

10/23

IF HE JUST LET THINGS COME TO HIM

If he just let things come to him
he wondered what would come to him
would the clothes in his closet come to him
drape themselves around him and button him up zip him up and
flatten his lapels would
full course meals come to him he wondered I mean
if he strictly followed the rule of *"let what comes"*

Would golden balls of light float in the air to him whispering
faint messages of reassurance and hope
would a sparkling white horse with brilliant stirrups and bridle
saunter up to him implying he should
mount it and let it carry him wherever it
may

Would the whole wide world open up to him if he really
put himself in such a saintly position with the
caveat that he should expect absolutely
nothing to come to him neither
sustenance nor wonder God's proof of His
Presence nor a revelation of same

That is if he stood on the shore of himself waiting for the
longboats to appear laden with coconuts and
butter or if he sat very still over a very
long or even short period of time to let

just anything wash up would it

he wondered be more of the same
the same hit or miss we get when we go out
looking for it or would it be instead
Lorelei and her mermaid maidens chanting delirious song or
hot rocks rolling toward us from the last
eruption in the far Caribbean

or perhaps a light lunch on a tray of like
whispers a few
soda crackers and a feather
the crackers to eat and the
feather as a reminder of Who the
Provider is after all for
all of it and how certain although

fleetingly and feathery in fact
all of it gets here

10/27

I FEEL A ROCK AGAINST MY CHEST PRESSING HARD

I feel a rock against my chest pressing hard
and I don't know if it's a meteor from God
or a chunk from Hell

It's got giraffes on it solemnly eating their
gorgeous golden heads pecking at high leaves

It's got rivers on it flashing pewter gleams
snaking between towns

And it's all very well to imagine it's the world but right now it's
pressing hard against me without
dwarf choruses or spectacular stairway dances
it's rough and dark and makes a rugged mile
it pulls me forward through a space that it
belongs to and that belongs to it

If there were some breathing room I'd be happy to let in
happy singing woodland creatures

If it allowed for any letup I might
sit on it as it rolls
so long as it rolled forward

It's got a pained expression on its rock face
which is the pained expression on my own rock face
as we wince along hoping for relief

If it's from God I'll let the pastures of praise recall
better days and see with tight vision
the open spaces within everyone *halleluiah*

If it's from Hell I fear it'll be with me for a while
unconquered by a smile

10/28

TEN THOUSAND LOVE LETTERS

Ten thousand love letters
(*the clouds look like a sea of icebergs from above*)
Ten thousand love letters to write
before I go

One to each flake and molecule of the giant
aerial milk pitcher in the sky whose bright
flow makes all our faces shine

One to each gaze of love across from one being to another
under Desolation Bridge eating civilization's debris

A few thousand to birds whose sonorous weave has
kept us well all these years
crickets and cicadas filling the silent nights with
a listening kind of rattle that
scintillates our ears
(*the roar of the prop plane below me vibrates my
chair*)

We're heading out to sea
and the sea is the sky
and the sky is the heart my hearties

The sky is the holy heart of us all
my hearties

10/28 (in mid-flight to
Fayetteville, Arkansas)

OUT OF THE FOXGLOVE

Out of the foxglove let flow delicate voices
out of the ocean-hiss let silence flow
out of bluebells an unaccustomed rattle
words out of the horse's mouth cantering in place

blasphemy from the harsh ripping of metal rivets out of girders
catechism from river-water flood call slosh and reply
karaoke from the sound of traffic rattling and honking at rush hour
high-C soprano note from a collective beehive in the rain
jackhammer presidential campaign speech
clank and clunk clank and clunk

high-pitched victory ululations kids leaving the schoolroom
for the playground
crinkly syncopated delicate percussion symphony autumn leaves
falling in a forest *tip and tap*
toads' preemptive silencing technique croak and counter croak
in the depths of night
a rolling penny on marble out of whose traction
whole marching bands cascade upward

Out of a ribbon's lazy rippling descent through the air
a light melody of languorous movement floating in space
from a steam calliope whistle the battle cry of giant sea vessels
erupting
from a volcano's gastric rumblings the sound of
wild stallions *en estampido* across Midwestern plains
at high noon

The voice of a charging fire across a virgin forest mountain range
as a young boy opens his mouth to try to express
his deepest inexpressible mystical experiences
to the one sympathetic listener on earth
whose reply is a long echoing mellow chord inaudibly sounded
in the open spaces between planets and stars

From the wail of a nail being driven into wood
the divine voice of the angel of death

From the sound of a leafy branch being waved through the air
multitudinous wings

carrying us home

11/4

A HOUSE SAW ITSELF

A house saw itself reflected in a puddle
as a beautiful maiden and its bricks and
wainscoting trembled to see such a sight

The riddle of existence sits before us on the
table in front of us like a Rubric Cube insoluble
and unsolved

A bridge started leaping for joy and the cars never could
reach the other side because of its ecstasy

A fire continued burning in the same spot until
it opened a pit in the earth and the laughter from
Hell could be heard on the street by the
astonished passersby some of whom
passed out

We never know exactly at what corner we take
the whole thing will reverse or show its
meaning side raw
*(a crystalline palace on a hill suddenly becoming an
elephant and striding away back into its
herd much to the consternation of the
king and all his courtiers especially after the
first cooling mud bath in the nearest
watering hole)*

But the denominator isn't always the most

common one it might also suddenly
ascend and the hunchback look around and
find he's a winged horse or the
poor match girl pick up a wilted chrysanthemum from a
grate and find she's now living on Madison
Avenue surrounded by fresh cut flowers and
grand pianos

A taste may form on the tongue that is the
icy grapes of Paradise or a sip even one
sip of its rivers of nectar enter the mouth
enough to transform us

A light may come into our eyes from our
heart that's never been seen in them before
and could illuminate the shadow-watchers in
Plato's cave once and for all

A string of phrases come easily to the tongue
from another realm altogether
in which zebras can easily be distinguished from the
shadows and the trees
and the rubies of our implicit wisdom be made out
in the darkness of our resistant blindness

O Lord to Whom we are not strangers
and Whose Smile illuminates our very corpuscles
with each step we take to You
You are the Opener to a way we never
dreamed existed nor yet imagined couldn't exist
where the magpie greets us in sibilant tones

and fruit on the trees makes subtle
xylophone music as we enter

and the house sees itself as a beautiful maiden
with all her lights on in all her windows

and a ripe beloved blossoms in every bed
just for us

alone

11/5

SINGLE FILE

Single file through a very small slot
everything and everyone goes
to Glory

Brush fires in the low-lying hills
the sky itself darkening but splashed laterally
with color unlike any ever seen by the
human eye

We go from one ocean to another having to
scrunch our shoulders together slightly as we
pass through the slot on our way
glimpsing only fleetingly both the
ocean we come from and the one to which
we are going

We wear a tropical hat with a feather
and are attended by
small furry mammals of utmost devotion

Nothing is particularly easy about our passage through the slot
except the distant lute music
and the number of red snakes (themselves only
two dimensional) who flee from us
as if afraid of the light of our presence

When we finally emerge into the ocean to which we are
going it is the same as the one we've

come from only lovelier
swans gliding in midair
rainbow-hued roses at our feet like
scattered stars

Nothing familiar yet everything
right at home in its pre-destined place
happy in the rotating bath of its
perfect nimbus

11/10

A CERTAIN SMILE

There's a certain smile that drifts down through the air
from very high up

Bridges span it between continents separated by oceans
it has no clouds and can be said to be

part of the air itself

It has no shadow and yet is made of something
more than light

There is simply no earthly equivalent either in
space or time

for though it *"drifts down"* it doesn't travel through space
nor actually passes *"down"* through time any more than it

"bobs up" or slides in from the side although in
some ways you could say it appears from

directly *"in front"* or even from
"within"

for it irradiates and totally soaks through its recipients

Some realize its arrival and their
hearts from then on distribute its largesse to

whomever may
others are not aware though it *"lands on"* them as

directly and completely
sinks down through the various stratospheres of their

own tubular universes touching
planet upon planet like seeds adrift just

awaiting its bright pollination

First one tentative sprout then another sprouts out
until there are tendrils

Large gliding birds cross their marshy terrains
cranes and herons extend their wings to catch

the sunset rays of the violet hour and fly
grandly into the dark

illuminating it once and for all
with their primordial cries of

jubilation and longing

11/11

THE PREDICAMENT

The predicament is there is no predicament
everything turns into a butterfly eventually
and takes off into the bluest of skies on the
longest of days

There are foghorns out in space as well
warning against floating debris
the very air turning around inside air causes that
unmistakable crooning sound that accompanies
weightlessness

The predicament is we're all still here on and off the
telephone to Divine Reality Who's
always at home so it has to be trouble at our end
causing the bad connection static on the line gradual fadeout
or we haven't paid our bill for one flimsy reason or another

Yet the radiant sky is somehow itself proof of simplicity
and the calling across seeming emptiness by one
angel to another more gorgeously arrayed than an Amazonian Lyre-bird
should finally convince us the way
seemingly out of nowhere habitable cities arise
with their rainproof rooftops and intricate wiring
streets that lead to places up hills and into alleyways
oceans that unceasingly lap the shores around every land mass

seemingly perfectly happy babies becoming serial killers
seemingly perfectly miserable babies becoming ground-breaking
nuclear physicists

the enigma of it all only rarely slowing down enough to
take account of its anomalies

But the heartbeat by God the heartbeat of us all
more predictable than the seasons
whose gyrations are more tumultuous than a beehive when a hornet's
wandered in
more prone to foolishness than a
so-called Third World country's revolutionary government
sorting out its priorities

Still the predicament from here is chugging puffs of
steam making lovely
whispery motions through the air like a loosely woven fabric so subtle
it actually
dematerializes as it unfolds
which seems to be the same for our lives
growing less and less substantial physically and more and more
identifiable inwardly as either

one who becomes a happy butterfly thoroughly awakened in the dream
or a drunkenly dreaming butterfly thinking it's awake but is actually

fluttering smoke in an updraft
scattering its precious wing-dust in the wind

11/14

DEATH IS THE BREAD KNIFE

Death is the bread knife laid athwart our plates
bread and butter kept separate until it
comes into play spreading
yellow smoothly onto brown

Death is the worm that smiles its wormy smile
as it wriggles suddenly from the soil
glistening in early morning sunlight

It's a motor left running somewhere in the background
we become so accustomed to we
don't notice as we go about our
tasks till it guns its engine and
roars into the foreground at last

Death is a winsome maiden with rouge cheeks and
two jugs on her shoulders
one belches billows of black steam gaggingly thick
the other aromas of bright green alfalfa fields and
rushing streams whose sweet sounds and scent intermingle

It's a blink and we're gone

It's a yawn and we've disappeared into it

It's a blank sheet of paper slapped against an icy fence suddenly
filling with script with flourishes especially for us
in perfect penmanship

The morbid wrap themselves in black and
make long faces squint and clear their throats

The faithful open their sheltered eyes onto the
real world and see sheets of light break apart
and showers of light descend equally on
everything bringing

joy to the slightest root
and hope to the flimsiest tendril

11/17

THE ROAR OF THE CATARACT

The roar of the cataract drowns out your
butterfly voice *O my heart* under
construction with one myrtle branch and three
singing doves

And far in the distance a single blue sky with a
flare in it so bright red its very bright redness sears the eyes

There's nothing left to say yet we chatter on
as the avalanche increases behind us
pulling the whole town down with it except for
a single crystal and two flies caught in amber and an
ancient filing cabinet full of
sensitive documents and dental records that will
come in handy for identification purposes
once the roar has died down

Yet they say the silence after a roar is
deafening then uncannily eerie then absolute
O my heart with your steep stairways going up and your
steep chutes going down
snakes and ladders *O my heart* the giant
advances and swift declines

One moment the empress on her jeweled terrace having
tea and cut sandwiches
the next moment floundering in classical floodwaters
avoiding eels and Corinthian columns

These apocalyptic occurrences take place either in the
overheated imagination or in busloads of Chilean schoolchildren
actually driving off a cliff under
suspicious circumstances

But Beneficent God knows each sparrow's fall
and the delicate bones of each one's ribcage
lifted in song

11/18

I FACE THE SUNRISE

I face the sunrise window with one eye open
a yellowing gray-blue square in a black room
my other eye squashed in the pillow
squooshy coverlet pulled across me in the cold
click-clack of the clock tick-tocking by my side
as the room turns golden

as everything in it pops up into golden view so
gradually the whole world given its daily
bath of illumined existence like a
blissed-out elephant by its mahout

the whole world and everything and everyone in it
given momentary form by the light-spray of
God's Light nothing else really
real but it as some die

their vulnerable bodies falling away
by bullet or arrow dipped in poisonous atropine over what's
real but utterly failing to acknowledge the
only Real that's Real when absolutely

everything and everyone else is actually
forced to acknowledge their own transparency to His
true Reality at last

11/23

AFTER THE HYENAS LEFT THE ARENA

After the hyenas left the arena
after the jackals and crows did their work
tiny angels in strings of lights came running across the
cruel red sand and their

laughter was like faraway trains drawing nearer
filled with wonderful apparatuses for measuring things that
always disappear from the obvious such as
snowflakes and rockslides to the less obvious such as

shoeshine stands misrepresentation which ultimately gives way to
truth in all its naked simplicity like a
spray of cattails in a tall blue vase on a glass
table in the rain

Our roars and gnashing of teeth finally become less
ferocious and more docile as yesterday's bleached
rainbows arch over into a fully
chromatic tomorrow

Our flights can't all be *away from* but some have to also be
toward
with wings as fluid as oil through water
into a perfectly lucid silvery-red light

The anxious mourner looks over his shoulder even as the
coffin lid is closed hoping no one will
discover his identity as the crowd presses around him

yet the newly introduced inhabitant of the
grave knows and the river of his
knowledge flows all the way to the sea
his enigmatic sentences there being perfectly deciphered

When one obstacle leaves another takes its place until
we're wider than any obstruction and a white wind blows
all around us
each heartbeat like the ping of a little golden
hammer on eternity's rim

each star etching its trajectory across our
most intimate sky

11/28

THE MOON'S IN ECLIPSE

The moon's in eclipse and the chairs around the edges of the room
wait up all night for their
inhabitants to come home
from their holidays in the clouds

Each chair casts the shadow of the
person who'll sit in it until
something new happens which is every
nanosecond or some other arcane
measurement only God knows it's so
finely held between two seeming nothingnesses

A wisp of light floats across a giant opening
a tiny feathery bit of fluff also floats by
there are hundreds of people who could say this better than I
millions of gardeners capable of tending the
most potent and delicate rose deep
purple flower whose enfolded fleshy interior hides even love's
mystery from itself in its down-sloping
couches of black velvet

The room is flooded with moonlight
black waves batter rocks at the base of
midnight's bleak lighthouse
triangular cloud-shapes pass so slowly all the
rest of the world appears to be moving backwards

I have stood on one leg for a thousand years now

and the closed lips of the sky resting lightly on the horizon
have just now begun to open

though I'll continue standing this way until
all the chairs are sat in at last by the
dazzling conversationalists of the stars

12/7

OVER THE YEARS

Over the years a tremendous transformation takes place
and I don't mean just the various pressures both
internal and external air pressures gravity with its
incessant pull downward on inner organs and jowls for
example it's as if

the body were being pressed between two sheets of space
in its free run and while it moves
forward at its rapid pace it is also being
pressed between these slabs and slowed down
in order to more precisely go in a direction
which is perhaps what earthly mortality with all its
cavalcade of perplexities is all about

until the inner body wants to open up this little
lacquered box with its increasing cracks and
squeaky hinges and step out onto melodious
light pads like lily pads afloat on a
glorious lake that shimmers in no earthly sunlight

all these veins and capillaries of biological necessity
suddenly become herds of migrating butterflies lifting up like a
multicolored cloud and heading for more
open territory in which to praise by the
mere adulation of movement flight and the
working of gratitude's powdery wings

12/8

A HUNDRED DAYS HAVE PASSED

A hundred days have passed the
honeymoon's over and I've
yet to reach my goal

Animals wander loose in the fields the pens need
repairing small
fires break out on the treetops and float in a cloud
above the lakes

The nights are the best
when distant pianos play repetitive
melodies on only the
black keys occasionally strumming
the inner strings

Pitch black nights that descend like
claustrophobia over the landscape but instead are
liberating
all the white birds who love to fly up
when it falls to test their parameters
turning as one at the last minute then
turning again like a simple thought all five
hundred of them in an
identical wavelength

This is the night of the death ten years ago
which shook us all and I
shudder to remember

I wanted to immortalize his soul with a
reasonable facsimile he'd
recognize and be proud of instead there's only these
seven trained horses and sheds full of
mown hay and no one can recall the
refrains and choruses to bring the
whole thing to life again

The moon is almost purple it's so white
and shines like a hammer blow

The coyote's songs rip the hearts of the
most cold-hearted to shreds how could
any dumb beast sound so desolate and
alone like the truth-telling equivalent of our
fraudulent human souls the yowls of
obscure grief and abandonment we ourselves
wouldn't dare express lest it
lead us to the abyss

Yet the nights are not so lonely after all
and intense light enters us fully and
when we forget we remember and somehow all the
cracks in our universe and all the
impossible imperfections begin to resemble
character lines in the faces of our lives more than
regrettable losses

I've long ago learned not to
rhapsodize despair as anything more than
ingratitude and ingratitude as merely the

harbinger of a difficult death rather than
the revisiting of the excruciatingly poignant
sweetness of this life in all its
opposite manifestations

even as a crackle can be heard across the
darkened fields of
smoldering fires and the

doors of the outbuildings
bang against their frames

12/14

A SENSITIVITY TO STARLIGHT

A sensitivity to starlight
has turned the valley brown

and the fingers of the newly born
swirl their imprint whorls in the

same curl as celestial bodies floating far from
home

Air unites us just as space divides us
we all breathe breaths until our breaths complete their

horizontal cycle going the full round
and death collects them in a golden cup to pour in some

far inaccessible place where mystery takes place
and crickets call across the night's abyss

12/16

GOD HAD IN MIND

God had in mind whatever He had in mind at the time
and so He created the wisdom tooth

He was looking neither to the North East South or West
nor up nor down nor laterally nor diagonally
so He created icy Alpine lakes and deepwater shrimp in the
darkest ocean murk

the cilia on the cilia on the cilia of a nearly invisible hair
wriggling on a tiny protoplasmic blob

and the perfection of blood clotting in a system in which
every microcellular mechanism must be perfectly in place
to allow for the animal sneeze
and the nictitation of a snake's eyelid

this train to Trenton on this track rocking gently
back and forth
as well as the man who's decided he's a jaybird and so
ruffles his arms back as if settling his wings

and looks at you with one cocked sideways
eye and tells you what he's seen

while circumnavigating this gloriously
glowing globe

12/18

THE CAT GETS IN BETWEEN THE COVERS

The cat gets in between the covers and
waits for me to come out of the bathroom and
get into bed

She's down in there and looks out through her
green eyes against black fur at me
when I finally arrive
and I wonder if she's really waiting and
listening for the door to finally open and me to
come out and slide underneath her
weight where she's hidden in the folds

if she anticipates with excitement since she's
crawled in between there and seems so to be
waiting for me to fulfill her bond as well as her
playful surprise

as we perhaps wait to be called to God's side
to have our heads stroked with divine good
fortune at last or
waiting between the folds and crevasses of our
days to be lifted out into the light by a
direct hand and given either
clear instructions or condolences and congratulations that we
got this far without cracking

our patience paying off
for the cover to be pulled back where we've been

waiting to spring our personal surprise and be
acceptable as she's

purring right now licking her shiny black coat with a
licky red tongue then curling
contentedly to sleep

12/19

BECAUSE

Because he began as a baby and will end as an old man
Because the rose has a stem and isn't all the way rose

Because the looming building casts a long shadow the squat
building a short

and we don't really see the faces of insects the way
probably other insects see them

Because there's a quantum gulf between the
human world and the insect one

and probably a flea doesn't appreciate the difference in
personality or spiritual quality between one

juicy arm and another in quite the same way
we do (although they may)

And because horses with wings are rare to the point of
impossible and flying ladders of shiny bronze that

take you to the higher heavens rung by rung
are more an apt metaphor than something you can

pick up at your local hardware store
And because even the highest mountains come at

last to a peak
and the deepest ocean rifts hit bottom after all

Then we can begin to appreciate not only the
utterly complete pattern of things but also the

occasional breaks in the pattern as when for
example a building in a forest fire isn't

burnt to the ground an elephant is
united with a boon companion after more than

thirty years apart in their respective
circuses or zoos and their trunks entwine in loving recognition

or a true cascade of purest love bursts in
cavalcades of purest splendor from seemingly the

marrow of our bones in a hot flood throughout the
entire system showing us the loveliest connections between

mouse and rainbow paper-weight and
train wreck door slam and baby born as the

whole cycle repeats itself in a new key enough to
shiver the deepest sleeper awake and the most

delicate moth to suddenly have the
courage of a tiger in sipping the most

inaccessible nectar

12/20

DREAM

This morning just before waking I dreamt
I was attending a very radical and aesthetically
magical theater performance and recall
various performers in black-and-white striped tall
hats and strange costumes with discs on their
arms like bracelets etcetera

Then suddenly they'd run out of text and there was a
halt while they wrote the next
scene and the audience was on the
verge of getting restless when someone handed me a
large African harp (a *kora*) with skin
body and thick strings like yarn but whose
notes were as limpid as light

and I recall holding it
backwards but I struck the strings and began
improvising a melody and also began
singing and the sound filled the theater and everyone
became silent to listen

and so it went for a very long time me
plucking and singing until the person typing the
play came to an end exactly as I
finished and everyone was profoundly
moved and I remember sitting in blissful peace and
fulfillment and three foreign men from seemingly a
Baltic country came up to me and

one said *"You're a poet"* and I responded somehow

and they went on a little until I said *"Let's get
on with it"* and so the play started up again with the
new words and I woke up

Recalling this dream later I remembered also one from
recently

a flying dream and I was hovering in the
sky above people and had a golden harp and
played its strings and the most utterly
gorgeous music I've ever heard came out and
flowed over everyone to their
amazement and joy

12/22

PULSE

I can feel my pulse in my fingertips
like a giant orchestral cello sawing back and forth
in time to the central heartbeat I can

feel like a ship's engine deep in my chest
evenly pounding thank God across the vagrant
thought-waves that slosh forward and back in

black and white or lurid color with jiggling or
soaring motions above the throbbing earth of this
body miraculously meshed together minutely with its

perfect fits of each cellular sprocket perfectly in place and
humming like a terrestrial body crossing some
imaginary expanse like a blimp or struggling

sea creature whose dimensions and perimeters are all
constantly changing only the face remaining
somewhat the same and the face not really

ours at all but God's

                                                            12/26

AT LAST

At last without brokers or pea-shooters
a moment lifts its head like a cast-iron
rooftop rooster turning in whatever wind to
crow in the dawn
scarlet light along a black field

We enter the Timeless Zone

What has often been reported to us and described
even down to the number of lifeboats and how the
row of cabin lights glowed above the
floating slabs of ice

But this is a glad catastrophe
trumpeting angels on either side their long slim
ethereal brass making a sound unlike any other
to herald a world unlike any other
where petals curl back to reveal an intoxicating center
like a gas flame blue and golden giving off an
unscorching heat that is simultaneously a
coolness to the eye and a consolation to the hearts of
saints and shepherds whose unruly flocks may have
strayed over hellish slopes in search of a more
inflammatory herbage

Somehow the mercy filters through every pore of every possible
surface and where there is a rippling it becomes smooth
where there's a cracking and creasing it becomes supple and soft

where there's an actual breakup and desolation
light uncurls its coils and unfurls across and
through it as if where an underground tunnel formerly
ran through dark rock now what was
concave becomes convex and a green hill of springtime light
fills with innumerable wildflowers like a rainbow bridge
over which we cross to a place without doubt

Every good is here every pause in tumultuous breakers every
stillness every hand dropped to the side in sweet relief
every conciliatory letter written but never sent
now broadcast back to us in clouds of forgiveness
that propel us across a sky that is
simultaneously a plain without shadows nor any
obstacles to cast them

Light fills the crevices
articulate light enunciating our particular joy
where description stops baffled by its own fluidity
while the *thing-itselfness* of the *thisness* of this
indescribable thing

just continues to give of itself like the
breeze of the first stanza who continues to
flow from its particular compass point to turn
the black crowing weathervane burst into golden light
home

12/29

FLESHY OX

I am a fleshy ox growing lank in the shanks
white flecked beard eye-wrinkles paunch

with a perfect tiny pewter figure of Narcissus
gazing through my eyes' pools to see his face

in such a way he catches day's light
and pours out supernatural radiance at night

but one serpent greater than the rest
of ruby jewels and jaded diamond vest

winds around unseen behind the light
awaiting the perfect moment to strike

12/30

I WONDER

I wonder if I've even begun or even if it
can be done
intimations of the rose stairway
the blam through this imagistic sideshow with all its hackneyed
carnival tricks except true elevation
the Ferris Wheel never goes high enough even though it
does go round and what circles
up circles down

I wonder if I've ventured even one inch out
into it or past it my own
habits well soaked in the creosote of protected mentation

and even thought itself dear page after page of thoroughly
rinsed concatenation
whether I've ever really taken off into the liquid turquoise
to a new world or the This-world's true wonder

which isn't just a nosing past the thick red velvet that
hangs perennially in its diplomatic folds

*(the rest of this poem is missing, as I must have felt it failed as a poem,
and tore it out of my notebook, my usual practice. But ironically this one
might have been getting somewhere...)*

TRAGIC LEAVES

Tragic leaves are not falling from the trees
they already fell

Bare branches arthritically stretch now spindly
above the days-old snow like wood whiskers of some skeletal

codger waiting for a pink youth to flash past in all this
very white and gray and darker gray and dirty

white to snatch it for its sensual rejuvenation
impatient for spring some fleshy pink body all

curves and warm pits of throbbing life as even
the earth below this crust is with deep

multi-colors red veins like lightning going
down into the clay and up again

Ancient papery demons playing invisible *Parcheesi*
in the backyard in the freezing cold

a demon dog steaming like an old locomotive with
wild red eyes and loud thumping tail

We walk out there to our peril
anything might fall

such as another world of shimmering cut crystal
and warm yellow light

right into this white dimension slicing straight down
like a guillotine

to set us all free

1/3

THE PRACTICE OF ECSTASY

The tea refused to stay in its cup
floating in the air like a dark sunrise

The space in the door refused to stay in its frame
and walked out around various people and things
providing a clear way *through*

Little buttons refused to stay up and down a lapel
and formed curlicue designs on the side plackets instead

A general ecstasy took over
no one refused its invitation to drop their usual
concerns they unstrapped them unhooked them unleashed their
terrible tigers let their harnesses go so the fiery
stallions of their usual concerns could run free

The light refused to stay put in its place and visited
everyone's eyes one by one and collectively

The wind refused to go in just one direction and so it
blew up from beneath and out from inside and
from the top down enough to loosen the hinges of
everyone's preconceptions

We strode out for the first time unencumbered with fixed
prejudices

A sound was purely itself in the great orchestral

swell of things
voices part of the ongoing saga from the
beginning of time to the present and
tunneling forward

Little tiny things refused to be overlooked and joined in the
general celebration

A shout went up in the air and continued
ascending

A blue ray fell through its center and turned it
to song

1/5

WINTER SCENE

Cold winter night blue snow crust on the ground
colors bleached out to only a few from the usual spectrum

even multicolored things in black and white now
palladiums of xylophone ice cabinets in a near dimension
suspended

just above ground level played on by angels using
devilish mallets to make long low echoing *plongs* of sound

reverberate among skeletal trees housing the few birds
left in their snow coats trying to snooze heads deeply

buried in wing-pits like tight
feather balls for a sport frozen in space the pitch

suddenly stopped in midair until spring thaw
when all will float freely in space again against

flittering green backdrops and uncoiling scarlet splashes and
a soft golden ubiquitous light even in the middle of the night

it seems with earth's blood flow pulsing so
youthfully again through the vision screen

and everything again like a golden
ocean in motion with all its leaping arcs and arches

not like the
present suspended animation of the silvery ice-world held in the

center of planetary star-space like a single round teardrop frozen on its
sad descent to nowhere from no particular

origination to no clear destination but dear God's good
pleasure through all His various weathers rapidly

shifting from hot to cold and
back again in our

hearts

1/7

EVERYTHING'S BEEN

Everything's been but is no longer here
giraffes have loped away their necks like pendulums

The dream's dispersed into a bus full of gypsies
each one slyer than the next
and they've taken their magical paraphernalia
leaving only skunk shadow and this
sense of being
left behind while the main attraction's moved on

This room with the light on and cat movement
water heater hiss and clock-tick
and a bloody left nostril
one eye stuck shut and a heartbeat like someone going
upstairs two at a time it

thumps like fish flopping at the bottom of a boat after being
hauled in from the sea
over whose waves flocks of angels like whales
glide with perfect weightlessness and
equilibrium through perfect skies in perfect
equanimity

1/9-10

THE RATTLES

The rattles of the *Third Arrondissement*
and the specific platoon of lost pirates
and the flouncy ball gowns of debutantes long dead
in glass cases along the windy boulevards
and billboards advertising raw sugar cane and
cane sugar in saucy sailor shapes
peoples' faces in every poignant human expression possible
from innocently winsome with heart-melting smiles
to jadedly decadent with penciled eyebrows and teeth that
gnash

Moorings and drifting boats
empty rowboats on moonlit waters casting long shadows
ripple and flip of fish-dribble in the silence
skeletal buildings in midnight darkness
peoples' shades moving perpendicular to
struts and crossbeams
empty doorways
the first speech of the day words like flares set in a row on a
black horizon
a throaty cough from somewhere far away
the endless itinerary of things only God can keep with any
accuracy

Each fly that takes off on its virgin flight
each condor sailing from its airy perch on high
circling and circling this dull America where
everyone walks backwards to keep from the pain of it

yet it looks with earnest eyes into everyone's face
with such unbearable love it makes the
whole body shake
such love as mud has for turtle eggs or
frog bubbles as light has for every shade
of darkness as only the open-hearted have for every
saint and sinner of us as we crowd together
under the flaming arch in a land of
bright blue sky
hoping for relief hoping for
the best

The look of love death has on its face and in its
fathomless eyes as behind the burning irises legions upon
legions of angels file up and down a spiraling
staircase carrying love-notes and bringing back
blessings and reprieves

The look of love death has on its face as it
bends close to ours and says words so
deep to our hearts there's no lexicon able to
carry them no definition of them in
any human tongue
words such as virgin forests in the earliest
mists of dawn have as sunrays hit their
floating dust motes and water drops

Such love as silence has for the
slightest sound which it so lovingly surrounds
each breath of mouse-baby each
tiny twig-crack and leaf-creak

Such love as sound has in all the roundness of it noise
and the silence it so lovingly surrounds

1/12

SMALL PEEPHOLES

Small peepholes the size of strangers
dot the boardwalk

and in front of each one on a sofa of sand
sits a magistrate

while seagulls strut importantly around
and these magistrates arbitrate

all day from sunup to sundown except
Tuesdays when they're rolled in their

wheelbarrows home to sleep which they
do for a whole day then

back again the next day arbitrating whatever
the length of hair the width of why the amount of

stress the hope a person's allowed from his pit

They arbitrate details on otherwise already
decided entities

but they themselves are fuzz balls beyond arbitration
and only one is named Shirley

I WANTED TO WRITE A POEM

I wanted to write a poem that would somehow
redeem all my previous poems from the
aerial flutter of papers through a kind of
air-shaft like so many ephemeral butterflies
with only white wings perhaps with single
alphabet letters on them but none really amounting to
anything like a sentence or coherent thought

so I called on a pod of whales for help though they really
were too massive and on their
way somewhere to offer anything more than a few
high-pitched squeals as part of a larger
oratorio which is somehow the
feeling I often get with these verbal
constructs that they only skim the
surface or even the depths but are still only a few
high-pitched squeals of a larger oratorio
on its way to balmier waters

so I called on a small bird that at
least hops and flies from branch to bird feeder to
rooftop and is at least in a
more containable physical package but it only gave me that
one-sided sidelong glance and
flew away

I next and none-too-soon either
turned to my heart which went *thump thump thump*

like the drummer in Louis Armstrong's Hot Five
and that did it

O still *be still* my cardiacal landlord my blood-sweeper
star-gazer my strong and steady underground

heartbeat like a galactic periscope
keeping your narrow beam intently fixed on God's

illumined horizon
you will see it all

1/25

THE CHOCOLATE ARMY

The chocolate army melted in the first sun
not a shot fired no one wounded only a
blob of delicious liquid antagonism gone to sweet

Such preparations for the battle now brought low
each soldier carefully molded each face sternly composed
clenching its teeth sucking in its chocolate cheeks

They stood on a hill such a
brave bunch but unknowingly vulnerable
when the hot sun of Columbia Syria the Congo
came out that morning full force
gaseous neon-orange ball sending out its life-rays

At first the soldiers wept
they saw at once the predicament of their position
their arms holding up the newest in death's technology
lowered at ever-deepening angles until their furious force was
pointing at the ground at their now wet feet
which were melting into the turf itself at an
alarming rate

The entire squadron began to droop heads
pitching forward shoulders sloping
the enemy was shocked to see such abnegation of
ascendant power so easily accomplished with no
effort on their part they
took the field as it were though they were

reluctant to actually take it

sticky chocolate pools in the tall dry grass now
hot sun beaming down over all

1/28

A POET IN A DREAM TOLD ME

A poet in a dream told me she had
too many bones

We were walking down a corridor
"Too many bones?" I asked

thinking at first it was what she
meant literally too many bones in her

body then thinking it must be metaphorical
for something

*"That's what they told me I had
too many bones"*

1/29

SPARKLES OF LIGHT FLY LOW

Sparkles of light fly low over a gray field
turning it to gold

If I wanted to write an ode to light
little needles and pins on a black marble table beside a
large tome on medieval philosophy entitled
"Sparkles of Light Over a Gray Field"

the silver needles and pins struck by long daylight rays from the
large window overlooking the garden
telling more in their slender shining
gleaming shafts about light than many a
weighty phrase

Also dappled horses kingfishers or hummingbirds
entering and exiting the light like happy bathers
wave crests baring their secret midriffs for light to kiss
in the remotest middle of the ocean of light when
no-one's looking but those ubiquitous
eyes of light from whose light all light transpires
including the gleam in yours

Sparkles of light over a gray field
like the eyes of an owl
that can see at night

2/1

ONE GOLDEN ROSE IS ENOUGH - 1

One golden rose is enough to change the
value of the bush

Everyone gathers round to see a flame
that's turned silver

When animals begin speaking by looking directly
into our faces with utter guilelessness eye to eye

and books' pages open with a sigh
melody floating from their words

and doorways take us with an intake of breath and
release us with a tiny puff of air

and hanging plants whimper if they're hung in the wrong place
and something keeps driving up to our door

to take us elsewhere

All of this intimating with its jeweled point sticking visibly
through to this side for the first time

that there's another reality besides car-wrecks
three-alarm fires and anonymous bodies found

mysteriously down by the docks
with lines like sensitive webbing of gold and silver threads

drawn all the way from the next world
to their final form in this

And as we walk down a simple corridor
it may be lined

with fiery horses galloping toward us through giant cresting waves
or row upon row of angels twenty feet high seemingly made of

translucent alabaster more alive than
anything on earth

The hearts of all of us on the tips of tall pine trees glowing like
small amber fires in which whole worlds revolve

one orbit sailing in a circle past another
God listening by our fervent cries for His endlessly outpouring

Mercy satisfied at our stumbling delighted
when we find our tiniest flaws and

try to lick them clean

knowing which sea the rivers of us flow into
gaining momentum as they go

The gate's always open
and though it's broken its opening is true

ONE GOLDEN ROSE IS ENOUGH - 2

One golden rose is enough to change the
value of the bush

Everyone gathers round to see a flame
that's turned silver

A brooding eye lifts from a brooding world and
looks for the first time at a

friend and sees the familiar facial characteristics not as
an evolutionary assemblage of cunning and deceit

in their slippery permutations
but another of God's orphans capable of

angelic actions on a limited field

The soul that's pulled
dampness around it for years

then one day flings open the black window onto a Spring
blinding in its Technicolor heat

And where there was
nothing there suddenly is something

though there is never nothing in this hauntingly
vast universe of stellar dust drawn into

sudden godly shapes by His Word on the
spur of a moment that may take

millenniums to grow

But one gesture upward in a downpour
may provide each ant with a Japanese umbrella

one lift of a face from being sunken on the chest
long after the formulas for monster-making

have been shredded

one room full of vultures that opens its
shades to reveal instead a traveling circus from

Brazil who specialize in gravity-defying acrobatics
and the materialization of wingéd horses out of a

single frog on a black pad
into a choir so sweet and coming from seemingly

everywhere even the barnyard rooster even the broken
chair takes flight to where

no world can collapse it into its frail constituents anymore
one determined wanderer in silhouette at the bottom of a sunrise

one golden rose on a bush of already
gorgeous blooms

one feather of light floating for days from a
passing flock

is enough
to illuminate the path

2/4

APOCRYPHA

"Apocrypha" means *"things hidden"* such as the
books of the Bible not included in the final
canonical works thus
books that to some might be even more
authentic but parked as if in
side-street parking garages fully gassed and
ready to go having even more of the
truth in them or at least
part of the truth

stacked in ancient golden jugs against an earthen wall
rich fumes emitting from wide mouths
dilating the nostrils of all passersby who pass by
even taking tales of the phantasmal wine to
other shores so that outlying island people know of those
jugs in whose lowest depths great lakes of
clear intoxicating liquid brew through whose

glittering channels great rainbow-patterned
fish swim looking for ways to the
central ocean even mermaids and mermen occasionally
chug by with their propelling fish tails
and rolled up manuscripts in their teeth in which
cryptic letters carry secrets even the main tomes of knowledge
up in the dry libraries don't carry

Thus these are the *Apocryphal Books* to be
read only by the forewarned that in so doing

their toes may curl in clandestine enjoyment or their
most rare hearts open as if the inner secrets of reality were sculpted
just for them

which in fact
they are

THE BELOVED WEARS AN IDENTICAL HEAD

The beloved wears an identical head to the
lover
takes it off and it's a miniature blue pony
or the perfect ceramic face of a Victorian doll
in late summer moonlight

The face of the lover identically reflected through the
warps and woofs until the lover
takes it off and it's a Creole fisherman the
nanny of the landowner or the great great
grandmother's grandfather who stood tall in
Iowa as the natives burned his homeland to the
ground or perhaps instead when the

lover removes his or her head it's the actual head of one of the
fiercest aboriginal natives protecting his or her heart and soul against
colonialist infringement who saw
golden light in ascending rings before his or her
eyes in which an eagle of supernal radiance rotated
signaling ultimate death and its postlude of
spiritually ultimate victory

The beloved wears an identical head to the
lover
takes it off and it's the lover's own past footage of heads and
glittering eyes stuttering past frame by incandescent
frame smiling back

There are swinging gates and incipient cyclones

There are Bermuda winds and Balkan rumblings

There are rifts and gulfs and tectonic plates shifting perilously
as the real head of the beloved is revealed to be
itself also reflecting the light of God but other than
the face of the lover who now must be reconciled to

more combustible excitements
hallowed moonlight on freshly unrecognizable features
the surprise of the real emerging from delusory
mists
like sitting too close to a waterfall and getting
drenched in its spray

The beloved and the lover two totally opposite
yet planetary creatures connected at the
aorta

One pump speaking through two ventricular chambers
the echo oceanic

and its higher-than-heaven reply

2/13

AND AFTER THE SHALLOWS

And after the shallows and after the
rushes of foam and the silhouettes
and the thousand pound flakes that fall from
Mount Zibora

and after the bronze winds and ice-storms of shaved silver
rip-sawing through forests on both sides of the reflection
when islands of more substantial turf float up as if
they'd meant to be among the visually represented
all along with their

hoof prints and floors of heaped needles leveraging out between
trees to deeper more inaccessible seas
whose restless heaving sounds could always be heard even by
those to whom none of this is available to their
senses
but at fingertips and toe-pressure the round earth presses

And after this implacable shadow passes
and darkness undrapes its heavy folds from the
cut-out leaves leaf by leaf with sunlight
spraying out from behind each one

And after the thousandth revolution with the
same white water-drops dripping as always in the
same black pools
through whose shimmering mirrors you can just barely glimpse
the tops of heads and faces and antlers and fur ears and

light-shafts making their
first appearances between trees

a sudden perfect pearl of light alone on a stem in a
spotlight of pure gold emerges

expanding in the air to the size of the
entire atmosphere

2/15

OVIDIAN TRANSFORMATIONS

The two-faced liar became a simple acrobat
eminently capable of flying between extremes one of which
might be on fire

The ruler-defier became a small
cozy fire glowing golden and crackling
deliciously among its embers gathered around now by
forest animals and friends huddling lovingly together

The red-faced anger-bearer became a
shimmering twist of pinkish light in an otherwise drab
rock-strewn landscape like a ribbon of
waterfall from a great height into a
basin of blood no just a
basin of clear water

The inveterate procrastinator became a
family of contented beavers slapping the
gurgling river waters with their tails and
patiently and methodically chewing and building
sturdy spans and cantilevers

and these are instantaneous Ovidian transformations
almost taking place at the moment of action
where a diametric opposite quality gigantically overcomes to turn
failure into success worry into worship loutishness into
love

Beetles are well-behaved in their beatific beetle
universe and nothing is amiss
while some folks turn bestial with vestigial tails
in a non-dimensional shaft and lope off on all
fours growling with vengeful slobber

And yet others turn on a dime from gross to growth
rhinoceros to rhinestone
glittering gloriously in a glade

gladdening all hearts who pass by
continuing to gleam long after
daylight has faded

away

2/24-26

WE'RE ALL AT SOME LEVEL OF INCOMPETENCE

We're all at some level of incompetence
even a cat sometimes makes a false step and falls
on all fours with a shocked
look on its face

The universe with its square blocks and tinsel ladders
myriads of details no one can adequately
comprehensively surround
its mathematics of this added to that its
gravity which slams one acrobat onto the mat
while another flies gaily through the air

Those ladders those ladders leading out of this pickle
one rung at a time one foot after another foot more or less than a
foot apart
there's always a larger light than the one we hold within
more Paradise than our leafy thoughts allow
wetter water bluer sky

And this person who walks before us
whose dimension encompasses our own with its
flashing eye and heart streaked with lightning
illuminating more of the landscape than
we'll ever know

2/26

AN IVORY WHITISH MILK-LIKE SWIRL

An ivory whitish milk-like swirl of no set
dimension at the core of everything

great funnel of creaminess
churning through our conversation the other day for

example

or through the two planes crossing each other's airspace only one
mile apart the day before

or the whale pod finding its pure way to a krill-bed in the
far arctic like an intelligent cloud

a spinning milkiness of light in eagle's nest and
anthill in the Seychelles or atop Mount Zibora

O my bland brothers my whispering sisters
an ivory whitish milk-like swirl

that stretches from one solar cosmos to
another where not even physical light quite connects their

multiple elegant orbits
and in your eyes mountaintops desert floors

reflected there and caravans and
pick-axe expeditions into rarified atmospheres

but the milk sea of Godly eternity in our
bones and corpuscles

a circling swirl
against giant winds like sails moving

intrepidly westward to reach
illumination before sundown

the sun itself spun in its sea
with lines of fiery birds pouring in floods from it like solar flares

horizontally

2/28

WE'VE ALL ARISEN IN THIS WORLD

We've all arisen in this world as the result of some
rather remarkable circumstances

from the golden plasma that laps at the shores of the sun
and the spangled rushing flood of night's shimmering velvets

and the continuous drip of dark genetic faucets from the absolute
first people seeing fern-leaf and cloud-shape for the

first time
making love for the first time as the earth

turns in its casual orbit for the billionth or so time
arising into these people at crosswalks this black boy on a

bicycle not more than nine already dipping and swerving through
traffic with a stern face I saw in my mind twenty years ahead from

now same serious determination negotiating what
crosswalks and traffic snarls and blithely

pedaling away

3/1

A FLY A GNAT A ROOSTER AND A KANGAROO

1

A fly a gnat a rooster and a kangaroo
decided they would go to meet their Lord

They set off one fine morning as the sun was
rising out of its inflammable basket

They sang a tune to keep them heartened on their
journey since they had to pass through country

rough and easy ragged and smooth raw and cooked
not sure at any moment of the

outcome and whether or if they would even catch a
furtive glimpse of their Lord

Since they were old pals they sometimes
consolidated gnat on fly fly on rooster rooster in pouch

and kangaroo making those long hops with
tail propulsion and long back legs like earthly levers

lifting them way above the earth and
forward

We shall leave them there for a while
and I shall go back to sleep

2

They had a long way to go
they *thought* they had a long way to go

We always think we have such a long and
laborious way to go to meet our Lord in this life

dips and twists and tragic or untragic turns fate takes to
either put our noses squash against the glass of it

or separate us far away so that it
looks again to us like the Emerald City shimmering so

far in the distance across the poppy field

Well the distance doesn't matter
but the fly the gnat the rooster and the kangaroo

had in mind travails on their travels and an almost
actually hopeless hope about ever actually arriving at

all

While at our elbows is the salt we wanted
at our fingertips the burgeoning wealth

at our eyes the flash and liveliness both
taking in and giving out

at our mind's root and stem the rolling
valleys of His splendid domain

and enemy whisperings in our right ears that
put them off and made them think they'd

never make it the gnat the fly the rooster and the kangaroo

I'm going back to sleep so God willing
more later

3

A funny hodgepodge of creatures all somehow
telescoped in this quasi-fable into one

long-tailed longing one energetic back-leg'd
hop forward in our valiant quest

I wish I could tell you it was a success
all I can say is

the rusted petals of a rose turn even water brown
while a fresh rose under the tap lets clear

gushes flow

A solitary tree on a hill houses winter birds and spreads a
snow umbrella for weasels

A rock on a topmost peak hit by sunlight
flashes as the eagle's sentinel

We live our lives obstructed by absolutely everything
even our bodies themselves like windows full of

fallen department store manikins with
stiff expressions and arms and legs akimbo

All our experiences every image imaged every thought thought
like taut strings strung with flags stretched from the

shadow side into the light side
but if we turn it all inside-out

so the ocean laps above us
and our feet like wings

O then the air is hallowed ground for the
soaring soul

and transparency the key to passing through walls
into the clipped garden where we find our

menagerie now basking for just a moment in the
sunlight of their quest

4

But our intrepid travelers our spiritual warriors

soldiered on and wended their personal as well as

collective ways onward with an ever-bright
vision of their radiant goal always set

before them even if it later turned out to be
well

other than *"before them"* in the spatial sense
or *"ahead of them"* in the temporal sense

And one fine day when the sun was just
hovering above the horizon like a fiery biscuit about to be

dipped in late afternoon tea
a white moth no bigger than the quivering

flame of its quest flitted into view in front of them
scatterbrained and twitteringly flying as if

drunk and slightly
singing to itself as descending sunrays

shone through its nearly transparent
wings

bigger than gnat and fly though much
smaller than rooster and kangaroo

more substantial than gnat and less high-strung than
fly certainly less earth-bound than nevertheless

twin-wing'd rooster and like a scattered kangaroo-thought
drifting zigzag across its marsupial mental sky —

"Where are you going?" the chorus of travelers intoned
"I'm going to meet my Lord" the moth uncomplicatedly

replied as if it were merely sashaying across from
one point to another

"Going to meet my Glorious Lord" and did a flip and
turn in lovely corkscrew motion in the

air in front of their perfectly lined-up noses
"But how can you so nonchalantly be going thus?"

they asked and expected an answer as rationally put
but the moth was already being illumined by sunset's light

and its little mortal body with the flowing
flapping sheets of its wings on either side like an

aerialist held by its skillful and compassionate white-tight-clad
Brazilian brothers standing on their high silver crossbars

*"I go from my Lord
through the Light of my Lord*

*to meet my Lord
in His Light"*

the moth replied

"and fearing no rebuff by my brash dash to a Merciful Lord

I fly as steadily as the
pen that flows with these words

as the sword in the hands of a master swordsman
as the midnight revelations of a saint at prayer

whose face has turned toward darkness from darkness and
drowned in such depths of darkness that he's

emerged as purest light utterly
essentialized"

and with that the moth turned once in the
air and disappeared

5

I'm fully awake now having
recently slept and yet don't yet

know what will become of this tale whose
plot is so thin and whose characters so

improbable
the gnat for insignificance the fly for

being rejected by all
the rooster for being dawn's

prayerful proclaimer and the
kangaroo for simple creaturely *panache*

yet the breast of humankind contains them all
while still in befuddlement as to its

divine destiny and resignation
how many have taken the journey and failed

have never taken the journey and succeeded
have never cared for the journey and fallen into ruin

or longed to take the journey and the
bright flame of godly absorption enveloped them where they

lay

Yet we go backwards within ourselves just as we go
forwards within this backwards world to find what

unworldliness insists itself as we listen at the
door of love inside God's endless waterfall of

singing waters all around us
as we go

3/9-10

TURQUOISE CUBE OF LIGHT

There's a turquoise cube of light in my heart
and inside it a rose blooms purple and pink
with some jaggedy halo-rays going off at the
petal-tips into zigzags of lightning

and a round hill rises up velvety green you'd think
if you fell into it its clover-dew freshness would
bathe your face and fill your nostrils with
alfalfa-sweet vapors to actually broaden your mental view to
cinemascope and you'd fall deeper and deeper into its
deep-down coverlet for at least an hour if not
an entire lifetime

or at least the lifetime of a quick glance in the
two-way mirror to check your haircut or the
rich texture of azure angels' wings like folding
screens behind your head in ascending step-like fashion
all the way to heaven

though your head also could be
just as easily on a person infinitely wiser than
you or a number of other salty visionary speculations

whereas your head is on only *your* shoulders as they
say though it would be truly grotesque
everyone with heads screwed on right but with no
visible necks
a kind of tortoise convention with everyone

"sticking their necks out" but not having any
necks to stick out

An eagle came and fed on the feud between us
flying with it to another
universe altogether where the greatest
violence is the closing of an eyelid

the drawing-down of the corners of a mouth

a hand resting on a knee when a
wave is called for

a whisper repeated over and over when a shout is so
urgently needed

3/22

VANISHED AWAY COMPLETELY

I always feel it could all just evaporate away at
any moment that it's on the
verge of evaporating right this minute that
some parts of it are already going and I'm left
with nothing or next to nothing
were it not for the divine adhesive

That I'm on the verge of losing it all and any
ability to capture it or typify it or even just
sing limp songs to it in my fashion with all their
stampeding horses and heart-pulses throughout them
golden or not a few forlorn lamentations or
jubilations

And then look around at a scarce and
barren place with some bent figures in the
distance combing through the debris perhaps to
complete the post-holocaustal picture
but even in its minute particulars life is
but a dream merrily merrily we row our
boat down and the breath of
death angels on our cheeks gives them that
peach flush

There's an abyss between us and what we see

Ghostly ships are coming into harbor
great sails are unfurling and it's actually

more universe about to vanish in smoke

As their prows become visible they're already
evaporating

And yet the earnest sincerity of good-hearted people
suggests a kind of permanence

A thing which is already disembodied and
subtle in nature
has more solid endurance and reality and
fills up the abyss with something more than
fantastic zoo animals
ibexes dik-diks creatures with
curlicue horns and beady eyes

Soul-stuff actually is of the permanent universe
while everything else is already half-gone
sliding like a paper-thin 2-dimensional kind of
magical slide sideways into
non-being so that what we experience all the time is already
mostly gone and in the
next moment has
vanished away completely

3/24

THERE ARE BIRDS ON TREES

There are birds on trees in the middle of the night
shaped like alabaster vases emitting vapors

Their song entrances even the most distant planets

You can feel remote space-winds
curling through the notes of their song

But now they sleep their wings silently dreaming
each feather-tooth zippering together with its neighboring feather
with a whistle-sound like tissue-paper combs
as the interplanetary winds wiffle through them

O every night is holy
a holy hush a holy darkness
enveloping the whole

The crystal city becomes black and its glittering panels black velvet

But above this blanket of blackness
suspended slightly as if a double-image just ever-so-slightly off
above every material entity we take for
granted as being solid

(just more clouds of light in various geometric shapes)

in a brilliant blaze of turquoise

sits a city of light

above the city of night

3/26

TWO OR THREE WISHES

It may take up at least two or three wishes to
loosen the bonds of the illusory self
clink-clank the dungeon-door slam that
rings like death through the entire castle
of fluttering TV images superimposed a thousand flittering on
top of each other

bright eyes faces mouths yakkety-yakking soundtrack from
Hell it clings like bad soap its odor a kind of
psychic *fels naptha* it won't go away the
illusory self like so much clothing on a
clothesline between bombed-out tenement buildings in a
dark downpour

So it may take two or three of the most
valuable wishes one for example for
vanquishing multi-headed dragons flared up out of
fiery seas their green scales electronic their
red schizoid eyes as their
craniums crash
down repeatedly on our heads though one good
glance from our innermost glancer would
be enough to seriously
disperse all their molecules into pure sea-mist and
whispering fire-froth

Or a wish to bring rain to a parched land etched like a scorched
moon a wish to flood a

drought with sweet relief after pent-up impossible
aches driven to extremes
alas
camel and horse skeletons sticking up out of dry sand

Or the last wish the third the most
precious the one
to be used at the
intensest point of despair when the
hinges of the illusory self the nails the tar the red-hot rivets
bolted twenty-stories high onto steel girders for
ultra-permanence would seem never to come loose

the wish to pluck little
children from death and feed all the
starving populations of the world
the wish to stem the tide of premature madness
warm shivers of cold-heartedness icier than Mongolia
irascibly grasping and indefatigably holding on

Finally dispersing the illusory self into the illusory atoms it's
made of
calming once and for all its multifarious gestures of approval-getting
grimaces and wiles
the iron bonds broken which were finally more fragile than glass all along
the illusory self made of spider-web after all
at last torn aside

To a small body-shaped empty room flooded with radiance
singing *Hosannah Hosannah*

rays like gold thunderclaps resoundingly
announcing with an utterly serene voice

victory over the illusory self by
vocal light audible energy sweet

elegance sweet
delight

God's Presence without shadow as He
takes a step toward us

still alive on
earth and the sea

crashes the shore with its usual
waves its usual

sea gulls

its usual stars reflected in its
usual swells the entire

sky in the sea's rippling mirror
the entire

moon in a single tossed water-bead
the entire mystery in a

wave

الله

INDEX

ABOUT THE AUTHOR

Born in 1940 in Oakland, California, Daniel Abdal-Hayy Moore's first book of poems, *Dawn Visions*, was published by Lawrence Ferlinghetti of City Lights Books, San Francisco, in 1964, and the second in 1972, *Burnt Heart/Ode to the War Dead*. He created and directed *The Floating Lotus Magic Opera Company* in Berkeley, California in the late 60s, and presented two major productions, *The Walls Are Running Blood*, and *Bliss Apocalypse*. He became a Sufi Muslim in 1970, performed the Hajj in 1972, and lived and traveled throughout Morocco, Spain, Algeria and Nigeria, landing in California and publishing *The Desert is the Only Way Out*, and *Chronicles of Akhira* in the early 80s (Zilzal Press). Residing in Philadelphia since 1990, in 1996 he published *The Ramadan Sonnets* (Jusoor/City Lights), and in 2002, *The Blind Beekeeper* (Jusoor/Syracuse University Press). He has been poetry editor for *Seasons Journal* and *Islamica Magazine*, and the major editor for a number of books, including *The Burdah* of Shaykh Busiri, and *The Prayer of the Oppressed*, translated by Shaykh Hamza Yusuf, and the poetry of Palestinian poet, Mahmoud Darwish, translated by Munir Akash, including *Adam of Two Edens, State of Siege*, from Jusoor/Syracuse University Press, and *Unfortunately it was Paradise*, from the University of California Press. He is also widely published on the worldwide web: *The American Muslim*, and his own blog: www.ecstaticxchange.wordpress.com, and his website: www.danielmoorepoetry.com, among others. He has twice been a winner of the Nazim Hikmet Poetry Prize, for 2011 and 2012. The Ecstatic Exchange Series is bringing out the extensive body of his works of poetry (the full list of the books in print on page 2).

POETIC WORKS by Daniel Abdal-Hayy Moore
Published and Unpublished

Dawn Visions (published by City Lights, 1964)
Burnt Heart/Ode to the War Dead (published by City Lights, 1972)
This Body of Black Light Gone Through the Diamond (printed by Fred Stone, Cambridge, Mass, 1965)
On The Streets at Night Alone (1965?)
All Hail the Surgical Lamp (1967)
States of Amazement (1970)

Abdallah Jones and the Disappearing-Dust Caper (published by The Ecstatic Exchange/Crescent Series, 2006)
Ala-udeen and the Magic Lamp (published by The Ecstatic Exchange/Crescent Series, 2011)
The Chronicles of Akhira (1981) (published by Zilzal Press with Typoglyphs by Karl Kempton, 1986) (published in Sparrow on the Prophet's Tomb, The Ecstatic Exchange, 2010)
Mouloud (1984) (A Zilzal Press chapbook, 1995) (published in Sparrow on the Prophet's Tomb, The Ecstatic Exchange, 2010)
The Crown of Creation (1984)
The Look of the Lion (The Parabolas of Sight) (1984)
The Desert is the Only Way Out (completed 4/21/84) (Zilzal Press chapbook, 1985)
Atomic Dance (1984) (published by am here books, 1988)
Outlandish Tales (1984)
Awake as Never Before (12/26/84) (Zilzal Press chapbook, 1993)
Glorious Intervals (1/1/85) (Zilzal Press chapbook, ?)
Long Days on Earth/Book I (1/28 – 8/30/85)
Long Days on Earth/Book II (Hayy Ibn Yaqzan)
Long Days on Earth/Book III (1/22/86)
Long Days on Earth/Book IV (1986)
The Ramadan Sonnets (Long Days on Earth/Book V) (5/9 – 6/11/86) (published by Jusoor/City Lights Books, 1996) (republished as Ramadan Sonnets by The Ecstatic Exchange, 2005)
Long Days on Earth/Book VI (6-8/30/86)
Holograms (9/4/86 – 3/26/87)

History of the World (The Epic of Man's Survival) (4/7 – 6/18/87)
Exploratory Odes (6/25 – 10/18/87)
The Man at the End of the World (11/11 – 12/10/87)
The Perfect Orchestra (3/30 – 7/25/88)(published by The Ecstatic Exchange, 2009)
Fed from Underground Springs (7/30 – 11/23/88)
Ideas of the Heart (11/27/88 – 5/5/89)
New Poems (scattered poems, out of series, from 3/24 – 8/9/89)
Facing Mecca (5/16 – 11/11/89)
A Maddening Disregard for the Passage of Time (11/17/89 – 5/20/90) (published by
    The Ecstatic Exchange, 2009)
The Heart Falls in Love with Visions of Perfection (6/15/90 – 6/2/91)
Like When You Wave at a Train and the Train Hoots Back at You (Farid's Book)
    (6/11 – 7/26/91) (published by The Ecstatic Exchange, 2008)
Orpheus Meets Morpheus (8/1/91– 3/14/92)
The Puzzle (3/21/92 – 8/17/93) (published by The Ecstatic Exchange, 2011)
The Greater Vehicle (10/17/93 – 4/30/94)
A Hundred Little 3-D Pictures (5/14/94 – 9/11/95)
The Angel Broadcast (9/29 – 12/17/95)
Mecca/Medina Time-Warp (12/19/95 – 1/6/96) (published as a Zilzal Press
    chapbook, 1996) (published in Sparrow on the Prophet's Tomb, The Ecstatic
    Exchange, 2010)
Miracle Songs for the Millennium (1/20 – 10/16/96)
The Blind Beekeeper (11/15/96 – 5/30/97) (published 2002 by Jusoor/Syracuse
    University Press)
Chants for the Beauty Feast (6/3 – 10/28/97) (published by The Ecstatic Exchange,
    2011)
You Open a Door and it's a Starry Night (10/29/97 – 5/23/98) (published by The
    Ecstatic Exchange, 2009)
Salt Prayers (5/29 – 10/24/98) (published by The Ecstatic Exchange, 2005)
Some (10/25/98 – 4/25/99)
Flight to Egypt (5/1 – 5/16/99)
I Imagine a Lion (5/21 – 11/15/99) (published by The Ecstatic Exchange, 2006)
Millennial Prognostications (11/25/99 – 2/2/2000) (published by the Ecstatic
    Exchange, 2009)
Shaking the Quicksilver Pool (2/4 – 10/8/2000) (Published by The Ecstatic
    Exchange, 2009)
Blood Songs (10/9/2000 – 4/3/2001) (published by The Ecstatic Exchange, 2012)
The Music Space (4/10 – 9/16/2001) (published by The Ecstatic Exchange, 2007)

Where Death Goes (9/20/2001 – 5/1/2002) (published by The Ecstatic Exchange, 2009)

The Flame of Transformation Turns to Light (99 Ghazals Written in English) (5/14 – 8/21/2002) (published by The Ecstatic Exchange, 2007)

Through Rose-Colored Glasses (7/22/2002 – 1/15/2003) (published by The Ecstatic Exchange, 2007)

Psalms for the Broken-Hearted (1/22 – 5/25/2003) (published by The Ecstatic Exchange, 2006)

Hoopoe's Argument (5/27 – 9/18/03)

Love is a Letter Burning in a High Wind (9/21 – 11/6/2003) (published by The Ecstatic Exchange, 2006)

Laughing Buddha/Weeping Sufi (11/7/2003 – 1/10/2004) (published by The Ecstatic Exchange, 2005)

Mars and Beyond (1/20 – 3/29/2004) (published by The Ecstatic Exchange, 2005)

Underwater Galaxies (4/5 – 7/21/2004) (published by The Ecstatic Exchange, 2007)

Cooked Oranges (7/23/2004 – 1/24/2005 (published by The Ecstatic Exchange, 2007)

Holiday from the Perfect Crime (1/25 – 6/11/2005) (published by The Ecstatic Exchange, 2011)

Stories Too Fiery to Sing Too Watery to Whisper (6/13 – 10/24/2005)

Coattails of the Saint (10/26/2005 – 5/10/2006) (published by The Ecstatic Exchange, 2006)

In the Realm of Neither (5/14/2006 – 11/12/06) (published by The Ecstatic Exchange, 2008)

Invention of the Wheel (11/13/06 – 6/10/07) (published by The Ecstatic Exchange, 2010)

The Sound of Geese Over the House (6/15 – 11/4/07)

The Fire Eater's Lunchbreak (11/11/07 – 5/19/2008) (published by The Ecstatic Exchange, 2008)

Sparks Off the Main Strike (5/24/2008 – 1/10/2009) (published by The Ecstatic Exchange, 2010)

Stretched Out on Amethysts (1/13 – 9/17/2009) (published by The Ecstatic Exchange, 2010)

The Throne Perpendicular to All that is Horizontal (9/18/09 – 1/25/10)

In Constant Incandescence (2/10 – 8/13/10) (published by The Ecstatic Exchange, 2011)

The Caged Bear Spies the Angel (8/30/10 –3/6/11)(published by The Ecstatic Exchange, 2011)
This Light Slants Upward (3/7/11 – 10/13/11)
Ramadan is Burnished Sunlight (part of This Light Slants Upward, published separately by The Ecstatic Exchange, 2011)
The Match That Becomes a Conflagration (10/14/11 – 5/9/12)
Down at the Deep End (5/10/12 –)

www.ingramcontent.com/pod-product-compliance
Lightning Source LLC
Chambersburg PA
CBHW020913090426
42736CB00008B/607